Wedding Planner

Things to do before we say I do

Copyright © 2018 Mary Choutris

All rights reserved.

ISBN-13: 9781726846462

Contents

Wedding Checklist	5
Quick Reference Contacts	10
Inspiration	11
Budget	28
Guest List	34
Venue	44
Ceremony	46
Timeline for the Day	47
Photography	50
Videography	53
Entertainment	56
Wedding Dress	59
Other Attire	61
Beauty	64
Cake	66
Stationery	67
Flowers	70
Transport	72
Gifts	73
Wedding Helpers Checklst	83
Engagement Party	84
Bridal Shower	92
Bachelorette Party	98
Bachelor Party	101
Rehearsal Dinner	103
Notes	106

Wedding Checklist

Task	Date completed
12 months or more to go	
Announce your engagement	
Pick a wedding date	
Set a budget	
Compile a preliminary guest list	
Choose bridesmaids and groomsmen	
Decide on a theme	
Book ceremony location	
Book reception venue	
Choose a celebrant / priest / minister	
Book photographer	
Book videographer	
Research wedding dresses	
Start planning engagement party	

9 months to go

Order your wedding dress and start fittings	
Select bridal registry	
Choose a caterer	
Book your honeymoon	
Shop for bridesmaids' dresses	
Choose wedding rings	
Arrange transport	
Order wedding cake	
Research and book florist	
Book musicians, DJs, bands, MC and entertainment	
Reserve a hotel for your wedding night	
Book venue stylist	

6 months to go

Reserve hotel rooms for out of town guests	
Order wedding invitations and stationery	
Finalize guest list and mailing addresses	
Meet with celebrant / priest / minister to discuss service details	
Update passports if required	
Meet with hairdresser	
Meet with makeup stylist	
Select groom's outfit	
Select groomsmen's outfits	
Finalize items on gift registry	

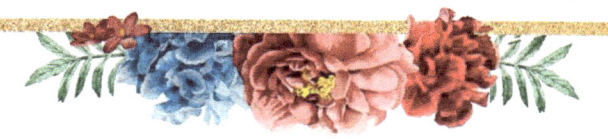

3 months to go

Give notice of intent to marry	
Send out invitations	
Start dance lessons if required	
Arrange vaccines for the honeymoon if required	
Meet with photographer to finalize location plans	
Meet with videographer to finalize requirements	
Request annual leave for honeymoon	
Start planning (or delegate planning of) bridal shower, bachelorette and bachelor parties, rehearsal dinner	
Arrange hair trial	
Arrange makeup trial	
Order favors	
Shop for bride's shoes and accessories	
Book your rehearsal dinner	

2 months to go

Shop for bridesmaids' accessories	
Buy bridal party gifts	
Choose ceremony and reception music	
Discuss final plans with the florist	
Finalize catering or choose menu at the reception	
Arrange seating plans	
Book final wedding dress fittings	
Have engagement ring cleaned	
Plan rehearsal dinner menu	

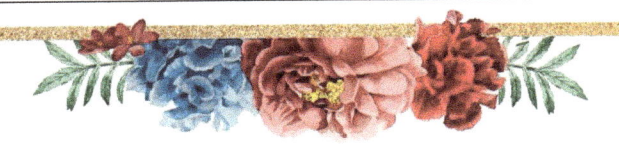

Buy lingerie	
Confirm all bookings	
Meet with MC to discuss requirements for the reception	
Buy a guestbook	
Finalize all wedding stationery	
Draft wedding program information	
Create running order sheets for ceremony and reception and give to relevant people	

2-4 weeks to go

Hold bridal shower	
Hold bachelorette party and bachelor party	
Pick up wedding dress	
Pick up bridesmaids' dresses	
Write your vows	
Give caterer or reception venue final head count	
Discuss music playlists with ceremony and reception venues	
Write your wedding speech or toast	
Start breaking in your wedding day shoes	
Pick up wedding rings	
Confirm all details with suppliers	
Book beauty appointments	

A few days to go

Give bridal party their gifts	
Pack for honeymoon	
Get manicure, pedicure and spray tan if required	
Pick up groomsmen's suits	
Drop off ceremony / reception accessories at appropriate sites	
Organize snacks and survival kit for the big day	
Hold wedding rehearsal and dinner	

On the day

Relax after all your hard work and enjoy!	

After the wedding

Mail thank you cards within 8 weeks of returning from honeymoon	
Send thank you cards to suppliers	
Change your last name and address if required	

Quick Reference Contacts

Venue:
_____

Celebrant / Priest / Minister:
_____

Photographer:
_____

Videographer:
_____

Florist:
_____

Transport driver:
_____

Hairdresser:
_____

Makeup artist:
_____

Cake baker:
_____

Other:
_____

Inspiration

Note your favourite Pinterest / Instagram / Facebook / Tumblr profiles,

Websites, Blogs and Magazines below.

Cut and paste your favourite items on the following pages.

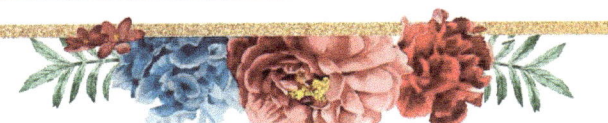

Dresses

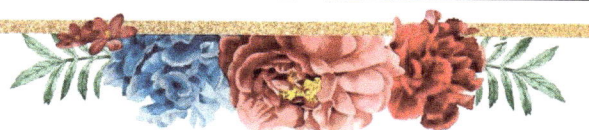

Dresses

Dresses

Dresses

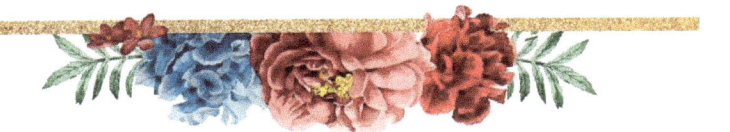

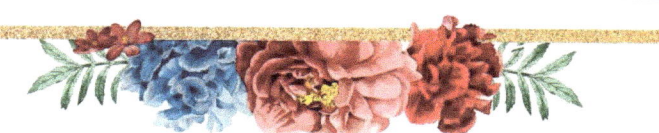

Make up

Make up

Hair

Hair

Cakes

Cakes

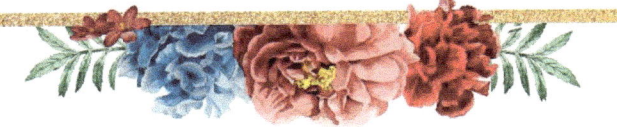

Flowers

Flowers

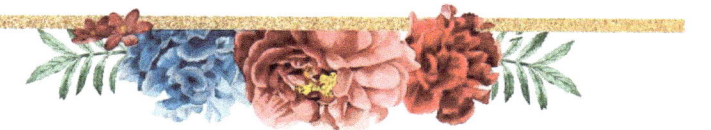

Venue Styling

Venue Styling

Groom's Attire

Stationery

Budget

Item	Estimated Cost	Actual Cost	Deposit Paid	Balance Due
Engagement Party				
Engagement Invitations				
Venue fee				
Catering				
Decorations / styling				
Bridal Shower				
Bridal shower invitations				
Venue fee				
Catering				
Decorations / styling				
Activities				
Bachelorette Party				
Party invitations				
Venue fee				
Decorations / styling				
Activities				

Item	Estimated Cost	Actual Cost	Deposit Paid	Balance Due
Bachelor Party				
Venue fee				
Catering / Drinks				
Activities				
Rehearsal Dinner				
Invitations				
Venue fee				
Catering				
Decorations / styling				
Wedding Ceremony				
Venue fee				
Decorations / styling				
Celebrant fee				
Reception				
Venue fee				
Catering				
Decorations / styling				
Bar / Beverages				
Wedding Cake				

Item	Estimated Cost	Actual Cost	Deposit Paid	Balance Due
Transport				
Bride and groom				
Bridal party				
Flowers				
Ceremony flowers				
Bride's bouquet and wedding party				
Boutonnieres				
Reception flowers				
Stationery				
Save the date cards				
Wedding invitations				
RSVP cards				
Ceremony booklets				
Confetti cones				
Place cards				
Seating plan				
Menus				
Favor tags				
Guest book				
Thank you cards				
Postage				

Item	Estimated Cost	Actual Cost	Deposit Paid	Balance Due
Photography / video				
Photography fee				
Prints				
Album				
Videographer fee				
Wedding video				
Music / entertainment				
Ceremony				
Reception music				
Reception entertainment				
Attire				
Wedding dress				
Headpiece / veil				
Lingerie				
Shoes				
Jewellery				
Groom's tuxedo / suit				
Groom's shoes				
Bridesmaids' attire				
Groomsmen's attire				
Wedding rings				

Item	Estimated Cost	Actual Cost	Deposit Paid	Balance Due
Beauty				
Bride's hair				
Bride's makeup				
Bridesmaids' hair				
Bridesmaids' makeup				
Gifts and Favors				
Bridesmaids' gifts				
Maid of honor's gift				
Groomsmen's gifts				
Best man's gift				
Bride's parents				
Groom's parents				
Favors				
Honeymoon				
Flights				
Accommodation				
Travel insurance				
Spending money				

Item	Estimated Cost	Actual Cost	Deposit Paid	Balance Due
Other				

Guest List

Name	RSVP	Table No.	Dietary Requirements

Name	RSVP	Table No.	Dietary Requirements

Name	RSVP	Table No.	Dietary Requirements

Name	RSVP	Table No.	Dietary Requirements

Name	RSVP	Table No.	Dietary Requirements

Name	RSVP	Table No.	Dietary Requirements

Name	RSVP	Table No.	Dietary Requirements

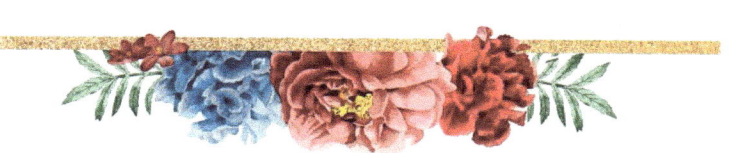

Name	RSVP	Table No.	Dietary Requirements

Name	RSVP	Table No.	Dietary Requirements

Name	RSVP	Table No.	Dietary Requirements

Venue Research

Venue	
Location	
Capacity	
Price	
Inclusions	
Availability	
Contact details	
Notes	
Venue	
Location	
Capacity	
Price	
Inclusions	
Availability	
Contact details	
Notes	

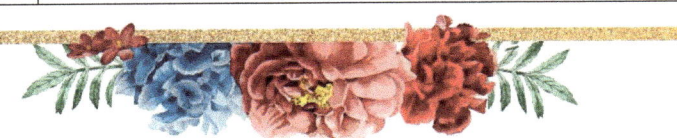

Venue	
Location	
Capacity	
Price	
Inclusions	
Availability	
Contact details	
Notes	
Venue	
Location	
Capacity	
Price	
Inclusions	
Availability	
Contact details	
Notes	
Venue	
Location	
Capacity	
Price	
Inclusions	
Availability	
Contact details	
Notes	

Ceremony

Ceremony Part	Person Assigned

Timeline for the Day

Event	Time	Notes
Rise and shine		
Bridesmaids arrive at bride's house		
Hairdresser arrives at bride's house		
Makeup artist arrives at bride's house		
Bouquets delivered to bride's house		
Photographer arrives at bride's house		
Videographer arrives at bride's house		
Hair and makeup to be complete and everyone dressed for photos		
Transport arrives at bride's house		
All to leave bride's house for ceremony		
Groomsmen arrive at groom's house		
Photographer arrives at groom's house		
Videographer arrives at groom's house		
Boutonnieres delivered to groom's house		
Everyone to be dressed for photos at groom's house		
Transport arrives at groom's house		

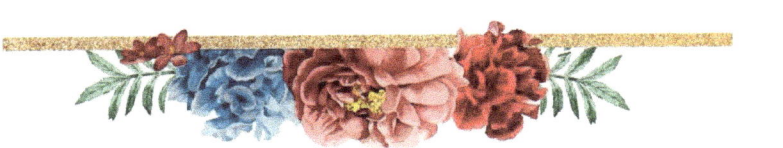

Event	Time	Notes
All to leave groom's house for ceremony		
Flowers arrive at ceremony and reception venue		
Photographer and videographer arrive at ceremony		
Ceremony starts		
Photos after ceremony		
Photos and videography at location		
Bridal party to arrive at reception		
DJ/ musicians / band arrives at reception		
Bridal party to make entrance at reception		
Serving of entrees		
Entertainment begins		
Serving of main meal		
Speeches		
Cutting of cake		
Bridal waltz		
Cake is served		
Bouquet and garter toss		
Event finishes		
Transport arrives		
Check in at hotel		

Event	Time	Notes

Photography Research

Photographer	
Price	
Inclusions	
Notes	
Photographer	
Price	
Inclusions	
Notes	
Photographer	
Price	
Inclusions	
Notes	
Photographer	
Price	
Inclusions	
Notes	

Photography Checklist

Note any special shots you require throughout the day, or photos with particular people you wish to have included as instructions to your photographer

- Wedding dress before you put it on
- Bride getting ready
- Bridesmaids getting ready
- Groom getting ready
- Bride with parents
- Bride with grandparents
- Groom with parents
- Groom with grandparents
- Bride arriving at altar
- Groom waiting for bride
- Groom's first reaction at bride
- Exchanging rings
- First kiss as a married couple
- Arrival at reception
- First dance
- Cutting the cake
- Bride with bridesmaids at reception
- Groom with groomsmen at reception
- Guests mingling
- Bouquet toss
- Garter throw
- Other:_____

_____

Photography Order List

Print item no.	Quantity	Price

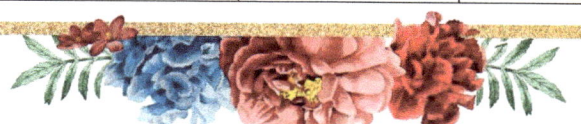

Videography Research

Videographer	
Price	
Inclusions	
Notes	
Videographer	
Price	
Inclusions	
Notes	
Videographer	
Price	
Inclusions	
Notes	
Videographer	
Price	
Inclusions	
Notes	

Videography Requirements

Note any special scenes you'd like filmed throughout the day, or particular styles you'd like to discuss with your videographer

Videography Music Selection

Song and artist	Section of video

Entertainment Research

Company	
Type of entertainment	
Price	
Inclusions	
Contact	
Notes	
Company	
Type of entertainment	
Price	
Inclusions	
Contact	
Notes	
Company	
Type of entertainment	
Price	
Inclusions	
Contact	
Notes	

Song Playlist

Title	Artist

Do Not Play List

Title	Artist

Wedding Dress Research

Dress name	Store / Designer	Description	Style No.	Price

Wedding Dress Fittings

First Fitting	
Date	
Time	
Deposit to pay	
Notes	
Second Fitting	
Date	
Time	
Deposit to pay	
Notes	
Third Fitting	
Date	
Time	
Deposit to pay	
Notes	
Fourth Fitting	
Date	
Time	
Deposit to pay	
Notes	

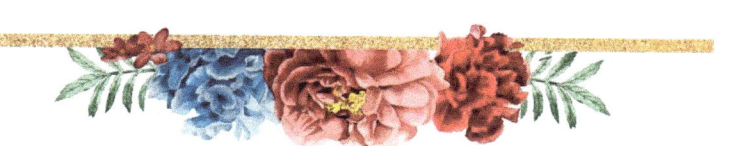

Other Attire

Item	Store / Designer	Description	Style No.	Price
Veil / headpiece				
Jewellery				
Bride's Shoes				
Wedding bands				

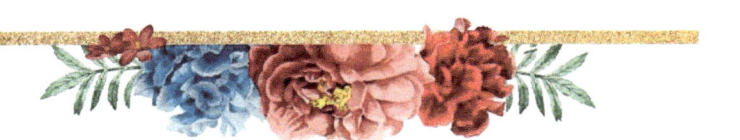

Item	Store / Designer	Description	Style No.	Price
Groom's suit / tuxedo				
Groomsmen's suits				
Groom's shoes				
Bridesmaids' dresses				

Item	Store / Designer	Description	Style No.	Price
Bridesmaids' jewellery				
Bridesmaids' shoes				
Others in wedding party				

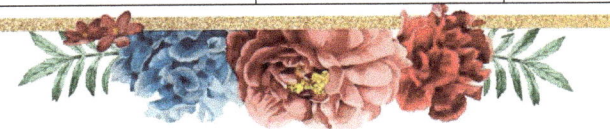

Beauty

Bridal Hair	
Salon	
Stylist	
Trial appointment date and time	
Final appointment date and time	
Description	
Price	
Bridal Makeup	
Salon	
Artist	
Trial appointment date and time	
Final appointment date and time	
Description	
Price	
Bridal Nails	
Salon	
Appointment time	
Description	
Price	

Bridesmaids' Hair	
Salon	
Stylist	
Final appointment date and time	
Description	
Price	
Bridesmaids' Makeup	
Salon	
Artist	
Final appointment date and time	
Description	
Price	
Bridesmaids' Nails	
Salon	
Appointment time	
Description	
Price	
Other guests' appointments	
Salon	
Appointment time	
Description	
Price	

Cake Research

Company	
Style	
Price	
Size and flavour	
Contact	
Notes	
Company	
Style	
Price	
Size and flavour	
Contact	
Notes	
Company	
Style	
Price	
Size and flavour	
Contact	
Notes	

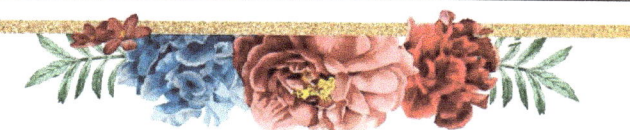

Stationery Research

Company	
Style	
Price	
Quantity	
Contact	
Notes	
Company	
Style	
Price	
Quantity	
Contact	
Notes	
Company	
Style	
Price	
Quantity	
Contact	
Notes	

Invitation Wording

Hosts:

___

Bride's and groom's names:

___

Wedding date:

___

Ceremony location and time:

___

Reception location and time:

___

Attire and special requests:

___

RSVP date:

___

RSVP contact:

___

Additional information:

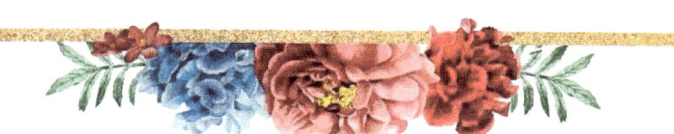

___

___

Stationery Checklist

Item	Quantity
Engagement party invitations	
Engagement thank you cards	
Save the date cards	
Bridal shower invitations	
Bridal shower favor tags	
Bachelorette party invitations	
Bachelor party invitations	
Rehearsal dinner invitations	
Wedding invitations	
RSVP cards and envelopes	
Ceremony booklets	
Place cards	
Welcome sign	
Photobooth sign	
Seating plan	
Menus	
Favor tags	
Guest book	
Thank you cards	
Others	

Flowers Research

Florist	
Type	
Price	
Quantity	
Contact	
Notes	
Florist	
Type	
Price	
Quantity	
Contact	
Notes	
Florist	
Type	
Price	
Quantity	
Contact	
Notes	

Flowers Checklist

Item	Description	Quantity
Personal flowers		
Bride's bouquet		
Maid of honour bouquet		
Bridesmaids' bouquets		
Groom's boutonniere		
Groomsmen's boutonniere		
Corsages for mothers / grandmothers		
Tossing bouquet		
Ceremony		
Aisle flowers		
Entrance way		
Reception		
Entrance		
Bridal table		
Cake table		
Table Centrepieces		

Transport Research

Company	
Type of car	
Price	
Pick up time and location	
Drop off time and location	
Notes	
Company	
Type of car	
Price	
Pick up time and location	
Drop off time and location	
Notes	
Company	
Type of car	
Price	
Pick up time and location	
Drop off time and location	
Notes	

Gift Registry

Description	Quantity	Price

Description	Quantity	Price

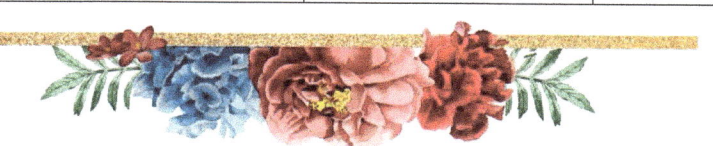

Description	Quantity	Price

Description	Quantity	Price

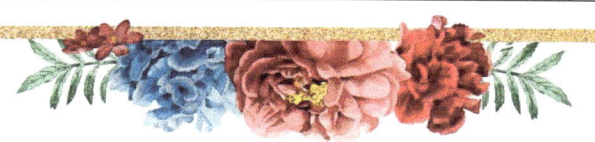

Gifts Received

Guest Name	Gift received	Thank you sent

Guest Name	Gift received	Thank you sent

Guest Name	Gift received	Thank you sent

Guest Name	Gift received	Thank you sent

Thank You Gifts Ideas

Maid of honor:

___

Bridesmaids:

___

Best man:

___

Groomsmen:

___

Bride's parents:

___

Groom's parents:

___

Celebrant:

___

Others:

___
___

Wedding Favors Ideas

Description	Store	Price

Wedding Helpers Checklist

Part of the day	Item to bring	Person responsible

Engagement Party Guest List

Name	RSVP	Dietary Requirements

Name	RSVP	Dietary Requirements

Name	RSVP	Dietary Requirements

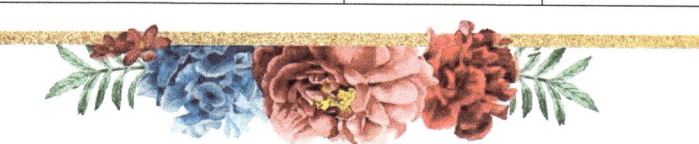

Name	RSVP	Dietary Requirements

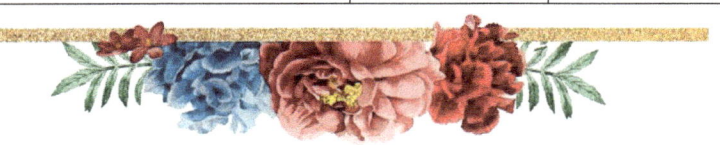

Engagement Venue Research

Venue	
Location	
Capacity	
Price	
Inclusions	
Contact details	
Notes	
Venue	
Location	
Capacity	
Price	
Inclusions	
Contact details	
Notes	
Venue	
Location	
Capacity	
Price	
Inclusions	
Contact details	
Notes	

Engagement Invitation Wording

Hosts:
_____

Couple's names:
_____

Engagement date:
_____

Location and time:
_____

Attire and special requests:
_____

RSVP date:
_____

RSVP contact:
_____

Additional information:
_____
_____
_____

Engagement Gifts Received

Guest Name	Gift received	Thank you sent

Guest Name	Gift received	Thank you sent

Bridal Shower Guest List

Name	RSVP	Dietary Requirements

Name	RSVP	Dietary Requirements

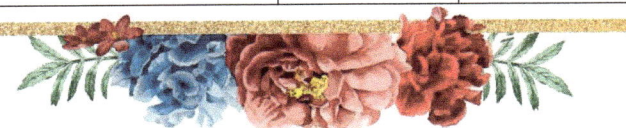

Bridal Shower Venues

Venue	
Location	
Capacity	
Price	
Inclusions	
Contact details	
Notes	
Venue	
Location	
Capacity	
Price	
Inclusions	
Contact details	
Notes	
Venue	
Location	
Capacity	
Price	
Inclusions	
Contact details	
Notes	

Bridal Shower Helpers Checklist

Item	Person Responsible

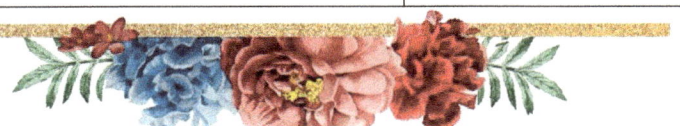

Bridal Shower Gifts Received

Guest Name	Gift received

Guest Name	Gift received

Bachelorette Party Guest List

Name	RSVP	Dietary Requirements

Name	RSVP	Dietary Requirements

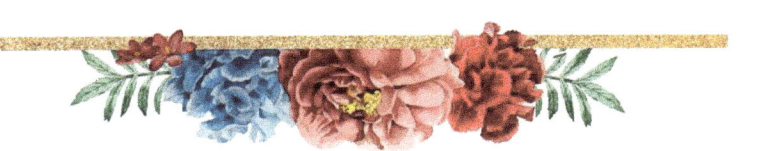

Bachelorette Party Helpers Checklist

Item	Person Responsible

Bachelor Party Guest List

Name	RSVP	Dietary Requirements

Name	RSVP	Dietary Requirements

Rehearsal Dinner Guest List

Name	RSVP	Dietary Requirements

Rehearsal Dinner Venues

Venue	
Location	
Capacity	
Price	
Inclusions	
Contact details	
Notes	
Venue	
Location	
Capacity	
Price	
Inclusions	
Contact details	
Notes	
Venue	
Location	
Capacity	
Price	
Inclusions	
Contact details	
Notes	

Rehearsal Dinner Helpers Checklist

Item	Person Responsible

Notes

Notes

Notes

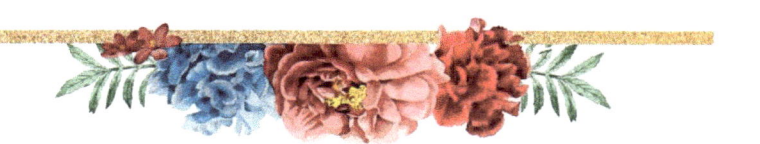

Ingram Content Group UK Ltd.
Milton Keynes UK
UKHW020922040523
421214UK00003B/12

9 781518 482847